It's a Ragtime Christmas

ISBN: 0-89898-321-5

Cover Art-Warren Conway
Calligraphy-George Ports
Paste-Up-Wes Middlebrook
Layout & Production-Ron Middlebrook

Y.O.T.B.

P.O. Box 17878 - Anaheim Hills, CA 92807
P/Fax (714) - 779-9390 - Email: Centerstrm@AOL.com

Ragtime is happy music.
Christmas is a happy time.
Therefore, play ragtime at Christmas.

Contents

'Twas The Night Before Christmas

by Clement Moore

Twas the night before Christmas,
when all through the house,
Not a creature was stirring,
not even a mouse.
The stockings were hung
by the chimney with care,
In hopes that St.Nicholas soon
would be there;
The children were nestled all snug
in their beds,
While visions of sugar-plums danced
in their heads;
And Mamma in her 'kerchief and I in
my cap,
Had just settled our brains for a long
winter's nap;
When out on the lawn there arose
such a clatter.
I sprang from the bed to see what
was the matter.
Away to the window I flew like a
flash,
Tore open the shutters and threw up
the sash.
The moon on the breast of the new
fallen snow,
Gave the lustre of mid-day to
objects below,
When, what to my wondering eyes
should appear,
But a miniature sleigh, and eight
tiny rein-deer,
With a little old driver, so lively and
quick,
I knew in a moment it must be
St.Nick.
More rapid than eagles his coursers
they came,
And he whistled, and shouted, and
called them by name;
Now, *Dasher!* now, *Dancer!*, now,
Prancer and *Vixen!*
On, *Comet!* on, *Cupid!*, *Donder*
and *Blitzen!*."
To the top of the porch! to the top
of the wall!
Now dash away! dash away! dash
away all!"
As dry leaves that before the wild
hurricane fly,
When they meet with an obstacle,
mount to the sky;
So up to the house-top the coursers
they flew,

With the sleigh full of Toys, and
St. Nicholas too,
And then in a twinkling, I heard on the roof,
The prancing and pawing of each little
hoof.
As I drew in my head, and was turning
around,
Down the chimney St.Nicholas came
with a bound.
He was dressed all in fur, from his head to
his foot,
And his clothes were all tarnished with
ashes and soot;
A bundle of Toys he had flung on his
back,
And he looked like a pedlar just opening
his pack.
His eyes - how they twinkled! his dimples
how merry!
His cheeks were like roses, his nose like
a cherry!
His droll little mouth was drawn up like a
bow,
And the beard of his chin was as white as
the snow;
The stump of a pipe he held tight in his
teeth.
And the smoke, it encircled his head like
a wreath;
He had a broad face and a round little
belly,
That shook when he laughed, like a
bowlful of jelly.
He was chubby and plump, a right jolly
old elf,
And I laughed when I saw him, in spite
of myself,
A wink of his eye and a twist of his head,
Soon gave me to know I had nothing to
dread;
He spoke not a word, but went straight to
his work,
And fill'd all the stockings, then turned
with a jerk,
And laying his finger aside of his nose,
And giving a nod, up the chimney he rose;
He sprang to his sleigh, to his team gave
a whistle,
And away they all flew like the down of a
thistle,
I heard him explain, ere he drove out of
sight,
"MERRY CHRISTMAS TO ALL AND
TO ALL A GOODNIGHT!"

Bring A Torch, Jeanette, Isabella

Traditional Provencal Carol
Arranged by Brian Dykstra

Gently, relaxed

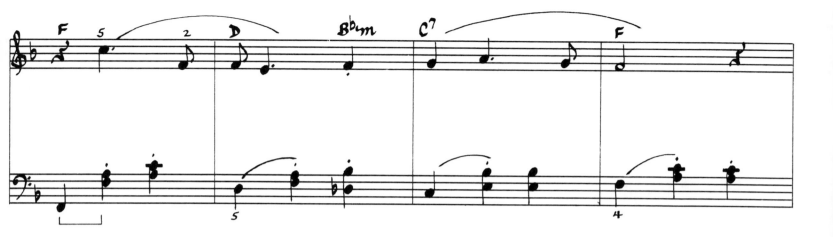

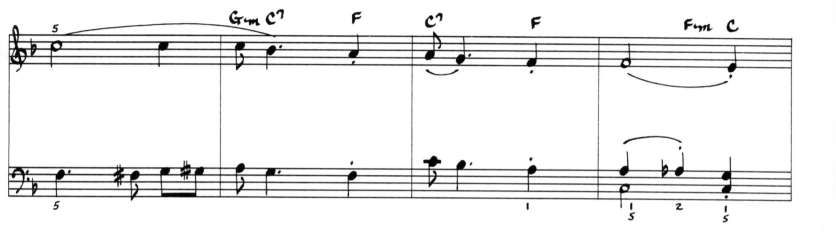

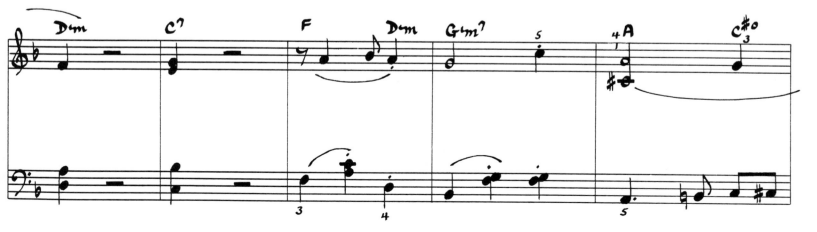

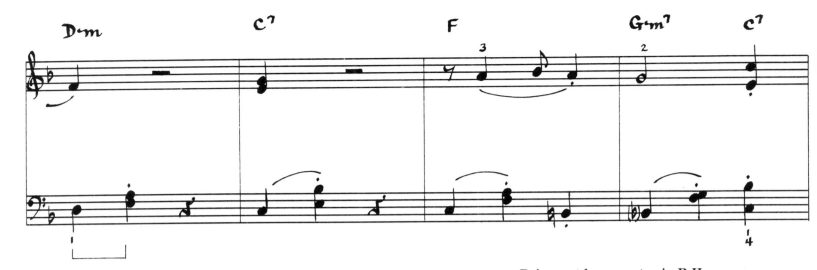

Bring out lower notes in R.H.

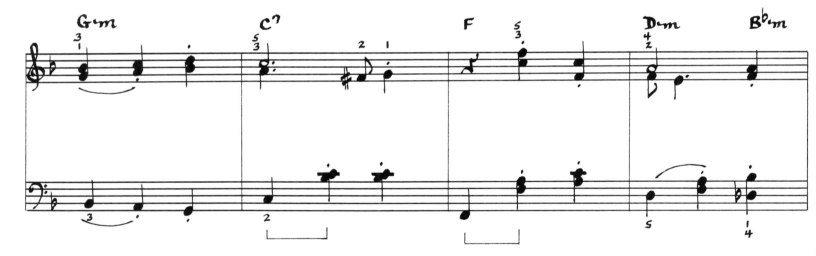

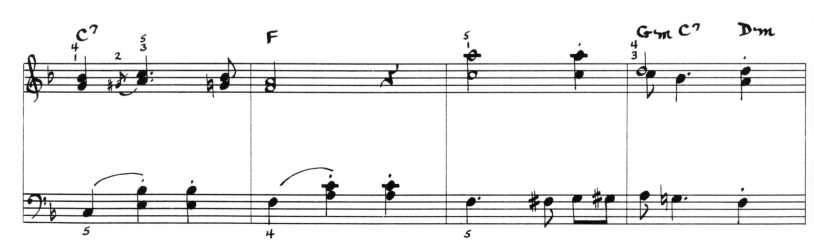

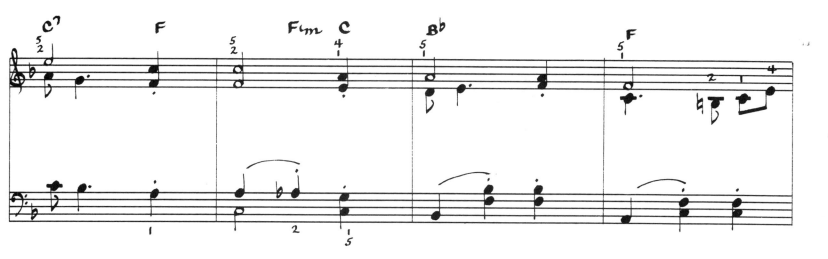

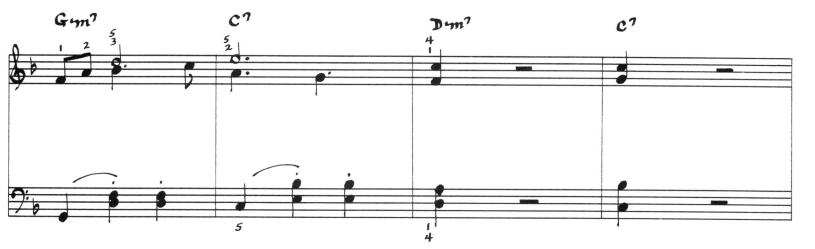

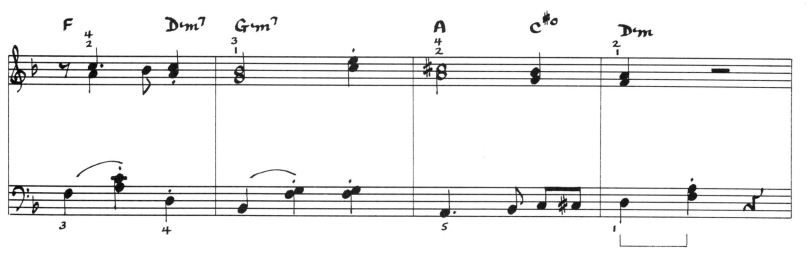

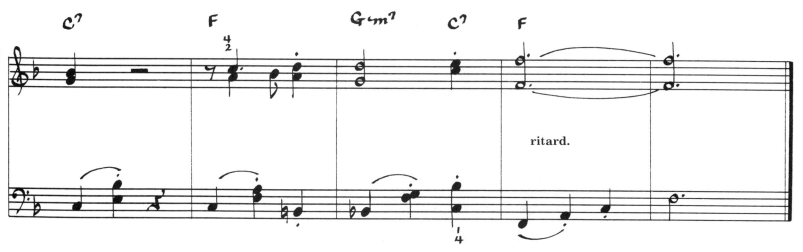

Bring A Torch, Jeanette, Isabella

1. Bring a torch Jeanette, Isabella.
   Lift it high o'er the crib in the hay.
   Lo 'tis Jesus, kind neighbors of Bethl'hem,
   Son of the Virgin Softly crooning.
   Lo, how stars shine so bright above Him,
   Lo how sweet sings the angel choir.

Deck the Halls

1. Deck the halls with boughs of holly, Fa la la la la, la la la la;
   Tis the season to be jolly, Fa la la la la, la la la la:
   Don we now our gay apparel, Fa la la, la la la, la la la;
   Troll the ancient Yule-tide carol, Fa la la la la, la la la la.

2. See the blazing yule before us,
   Fa la la la la, la la la la;
   Strike the harp and join the chorus,
   Fa la la la la, la la la la.
   Follow me in merry measure,
   Fa la la, la la la, la la la
   While I tell of Yuletide treasure,
   Fa la la la la, la la la la.

3. Fast away the old year passes,
   Fa la la la la, la la la la;
   Hail the New Year, lads and lasses,
   Fa la la la la, la la la la.
   Sing we joyous, all together,
   Fa la la, la la la, la la la;
   Heedless of the wind and weather,
   Fa la la la la, la la la la.

Deck The Halls

Traditional Welsh Carol
Arranged by Brian Dykstra

Gaily

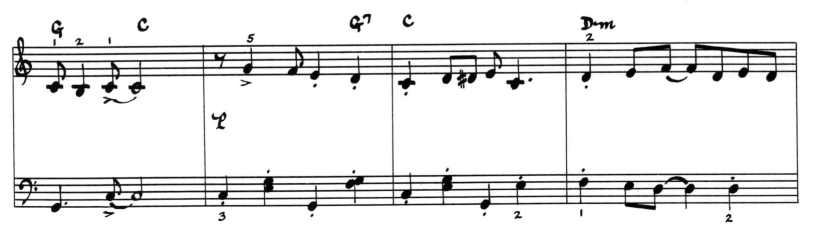

This arrangement Copyright © 1984 by CENTERSTREAM Publishing
P.O. Box 5052 Fullerton CA 92635

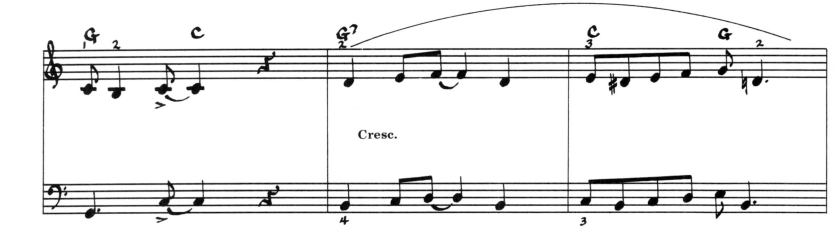

Cresc.

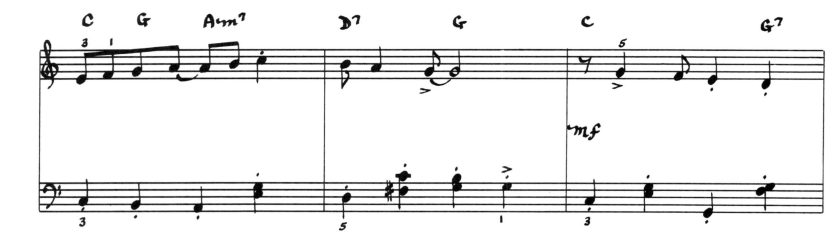

mf

f

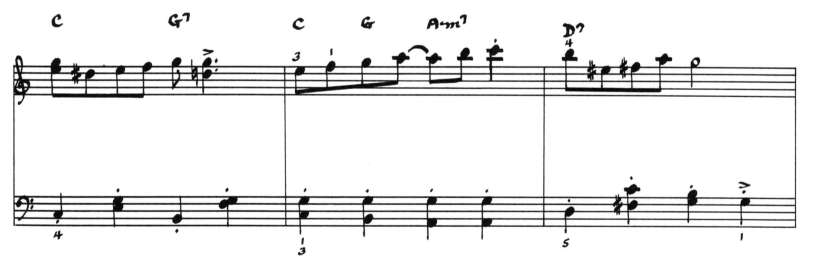

God Rest You Merry, Gentlemen

Traditional English Carol
Arranged by Brian Dykstra

Merrily

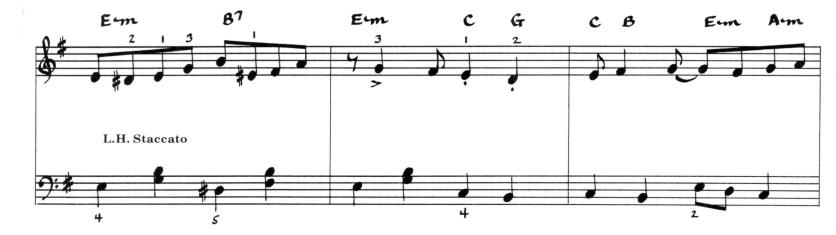

P. O. Box 5052 Fullerton CA 92635

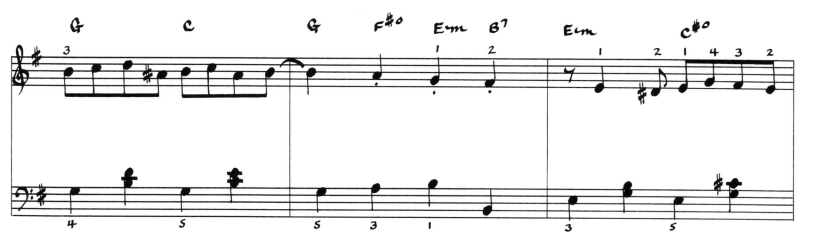

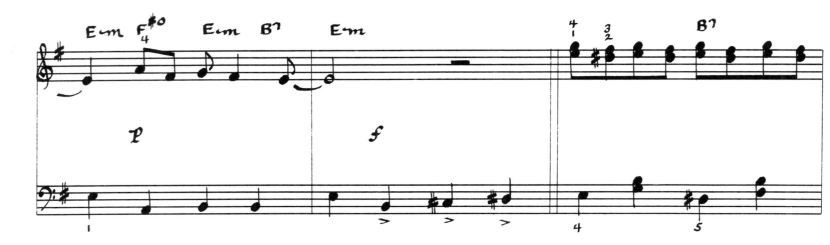

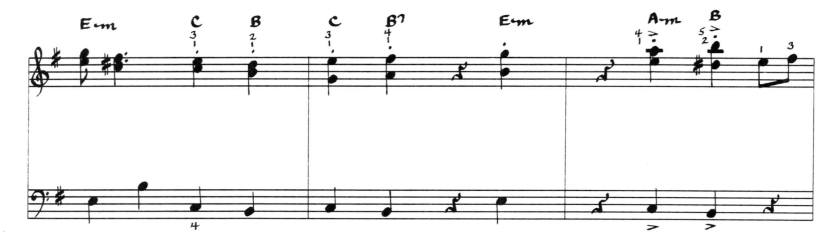

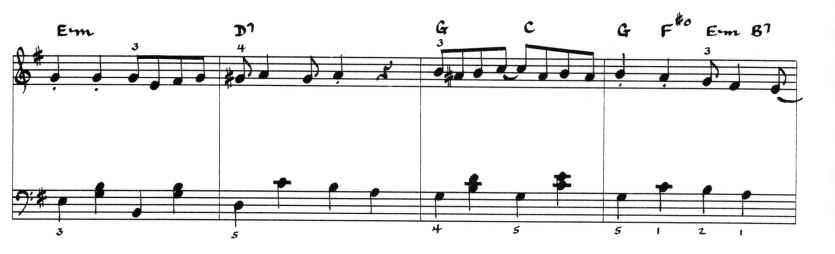

God Rest Ye Merry Gentlemen

1. God rest ye merry gentlemen,
   Let nothing you dismay;
   Remember Christ, our Saviour,
   Was born on Christmas day,
   To save us all from Satan's pow'r
   When we were gone a stray:

   Refrain:
   O tidings of comfort and joy
   comfort and joy
   O tidings of comfort and joy

2. In Bethlehem in Jewry
   This blessed Babe was born,
   And laid within a manger
   Upon this blessed morn;
   The which His mother, Mary,
   Did nothing take in scorn: Refrain:

3. From God, our heav'nly Father
   A blessed angel came,
   And unto certain shepherds
   Brought tidings of the same,
   How that in Bethlehem was born
   The Son of God by name: Refrain:

4. "Fear not," then said the angel,
   "Let nothing you affright,
   This day is born a Saviour
   Of virtue, pow'r and might;
   So frequently to vanquish all
   The friends of Satan quite:" Refrain:

5. The shepherds at those tidings
   Rejoiced much in mind,
   And left their flocks a-feeding,
   In tempest, storm and wind,
   And went to Bethlehem straightway
   This blessed Babe to find: Refrain:

Jingle Bells

1. Dashing through the snow
   In a one horse open sleigh,
   O'er the fields we go,
   Laughing all the way;
   Bells on Bobtail ring,
   Making spirits bright,
   What fun it is to ride and sing
   A sleighing song tonight!

   Refrain:
   Jingle bells, jingle bells
   Jingle all the way!
   Oh what fun it is to ride
   In a one horse open sleigh!
   (repeat)

2. A day or two ago,
   I thought I'd take a ride,
   And soon Miss Fanny Bright
   Was seated by my side;
   The horse was lean and lank;
   Misfortune seemed his lot;
   He got into a drifted bank,
   And we, we got upsot. Refrain:

3. A day or two ago,
   The story I must tell
   I went out on the snow
   And on my back I fell;
   A gent was riding by
   In a one-horse open sleigh,
   He laughed as there I sprawling lie,
   But quickly drove away. Refrain:

4. Now the ground is white
   Go it while you're young,
   Take the girls tonight
   And sing this sleighing song;
   Just get a bobtailed bay
   Two-forty as his speed
   Hitch him to an open sleigh
   And crack! you'll take the lead.

Jingle Bells

With Bright Spirits

James Pierpont
Arranged by Brian Dykstra

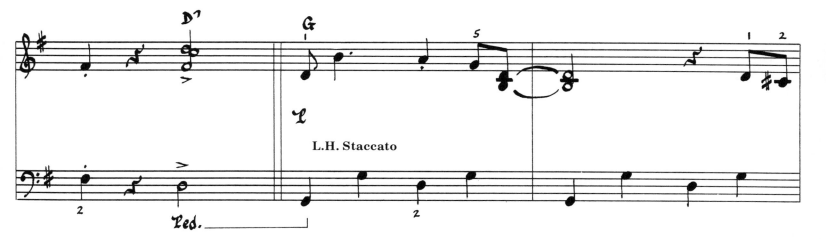

L.H. Staccato

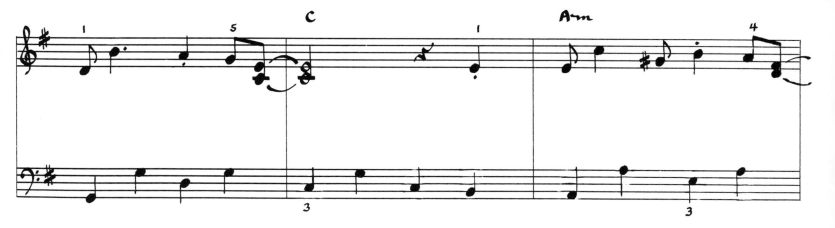

P. O. Box 5052 Fullerton CA 92635

17

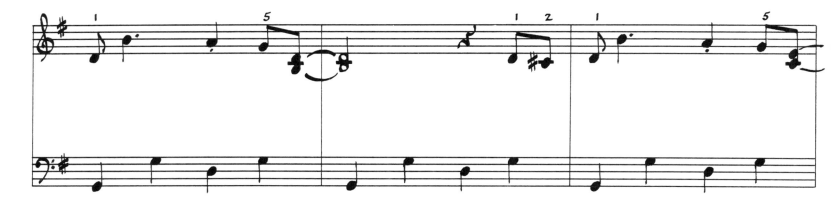

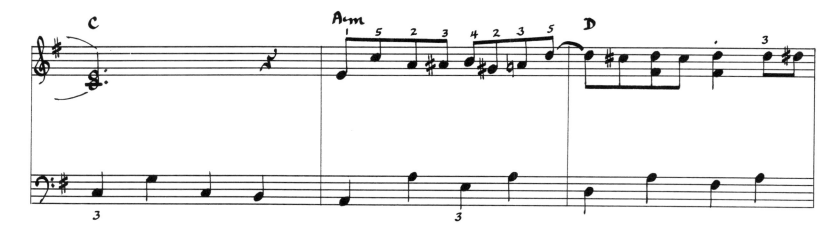

18

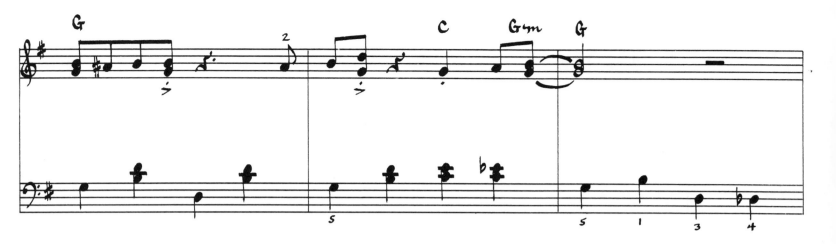

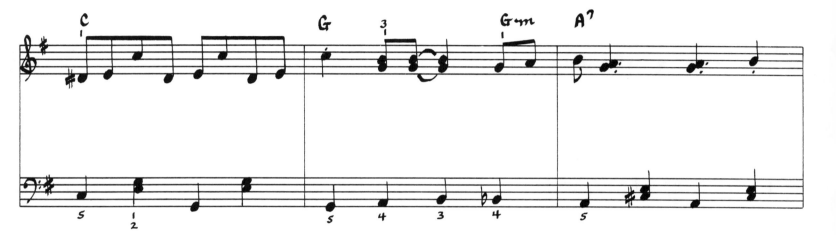

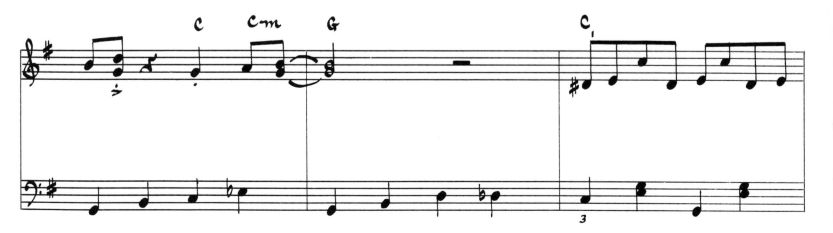

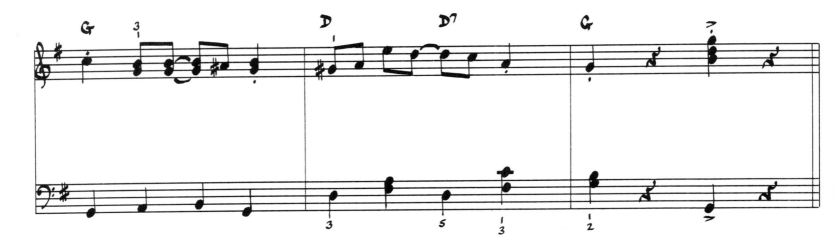

Cresc.

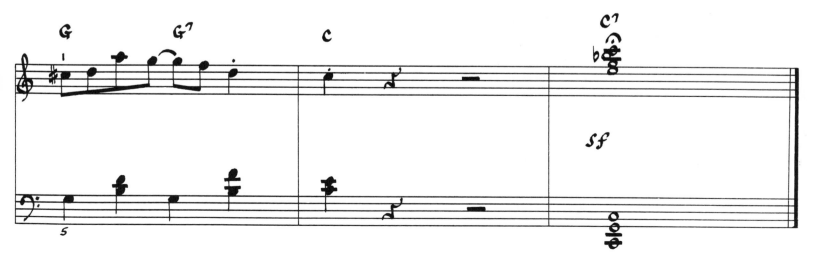

Jolly Old St. Nicholas

Traditional American Carol
Arranged by Brian Dykstra

Jolly

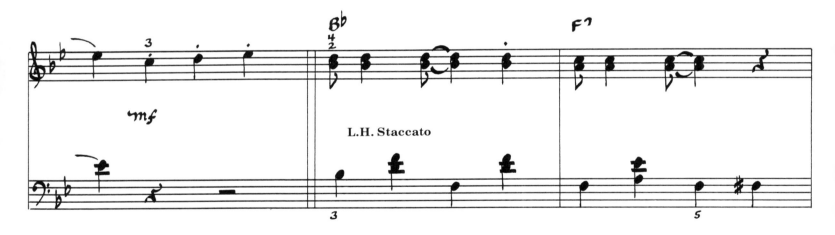

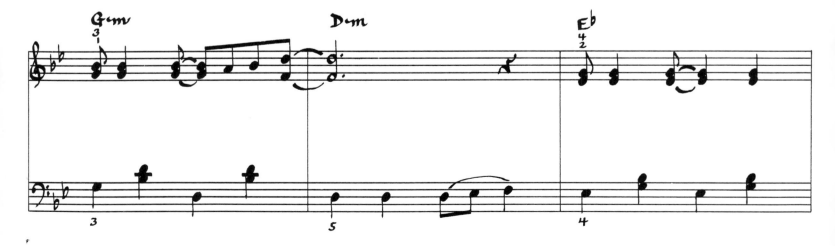

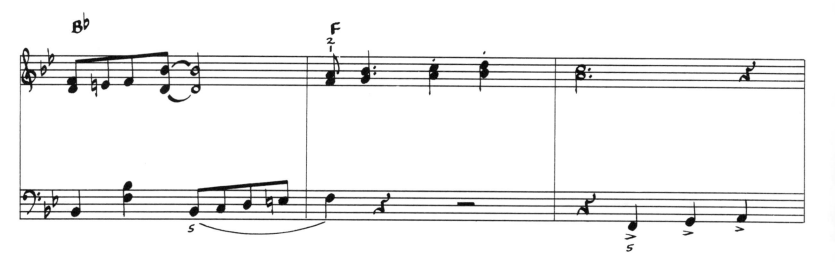

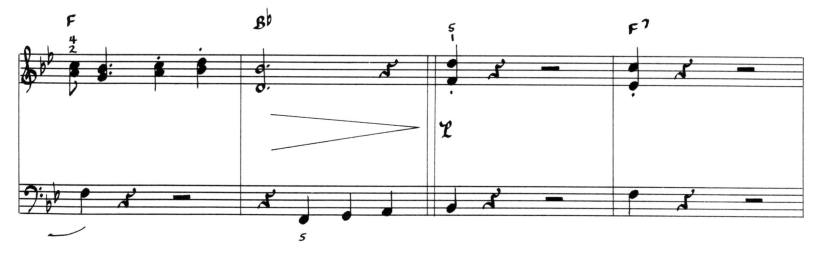

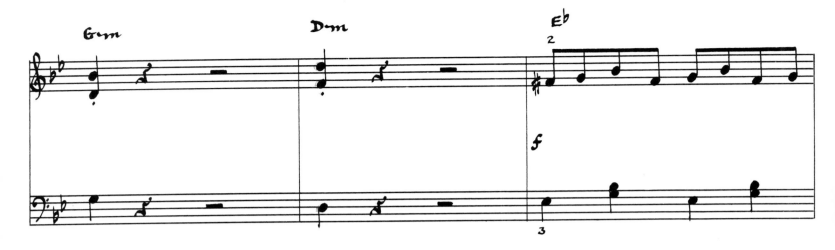

Jolly Old St. Nicholas

1. Jolly old Saint Nicholas,
    lean your ear this way!
    Don't you tell a single soul
    what I'm going to say;
    Christmas Eve is coming soon;
    now you dear old man,
    Whisper what you'll bring to me;
    Tell me if you can.

O Christmas Tree

1. O Christmas tree, O Christmas tree,
    with faithful leaves unchanging.
    O Christmas tree, O Christmas tree.
    with faithful leaves unchanging;
    Not only green in summer's heat,
    But also winter's snow and sleet,
    O Christmas tree, O Christmas tree,
    with faithful leaves unchanging.

O Christmas Tree

Traditional German Carol
Arranged by Brian Dykstra

Joyously

L.H. Staccato

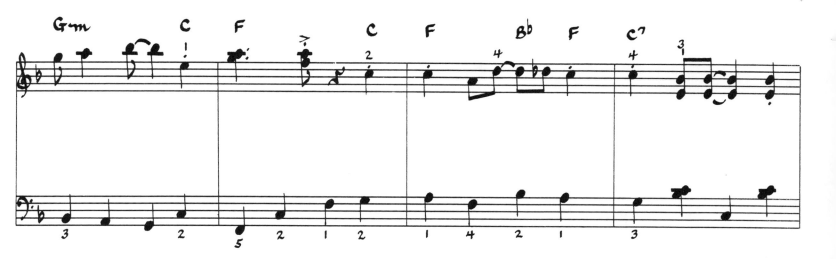

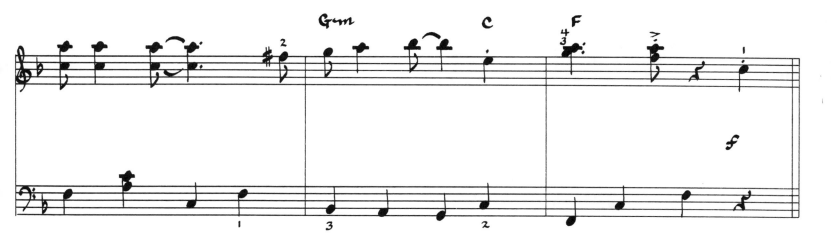

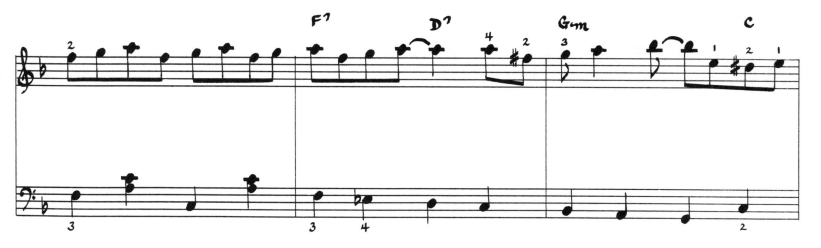

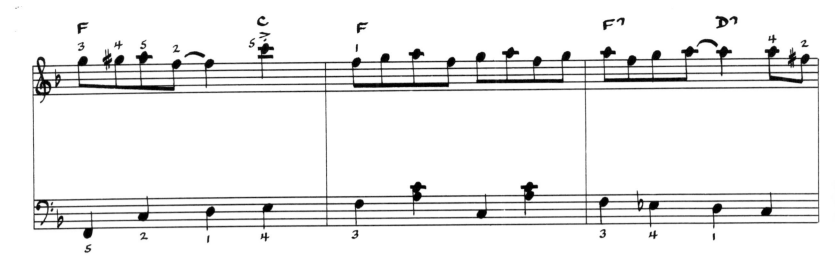

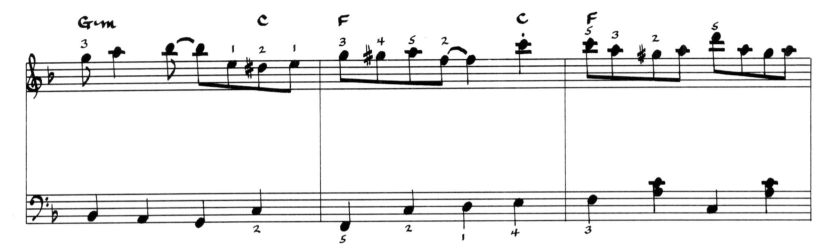

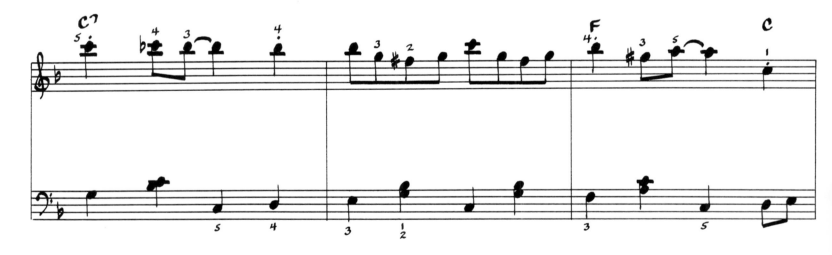

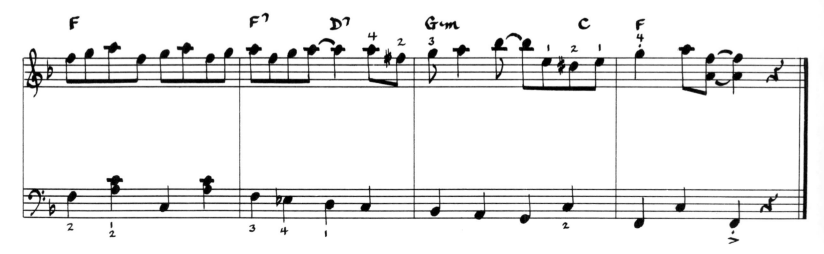

The Twelve Days Of Christmas

Traditional English Carol
Arranged by Brian Dykstra

Cheerily

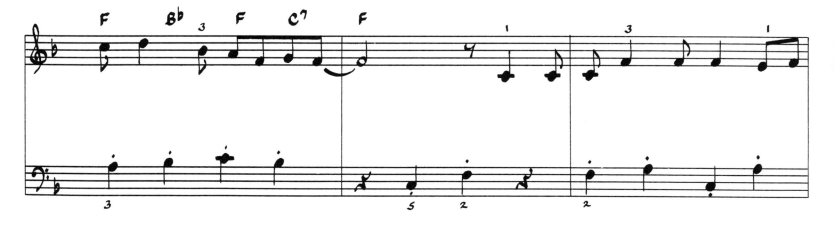

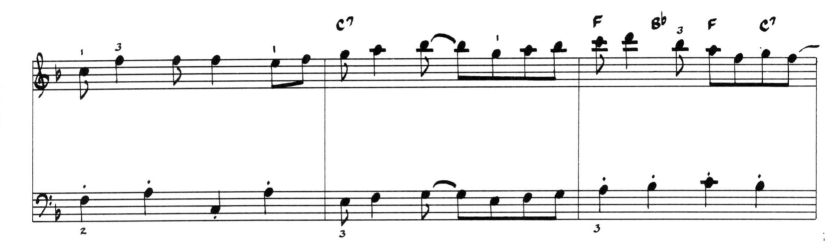

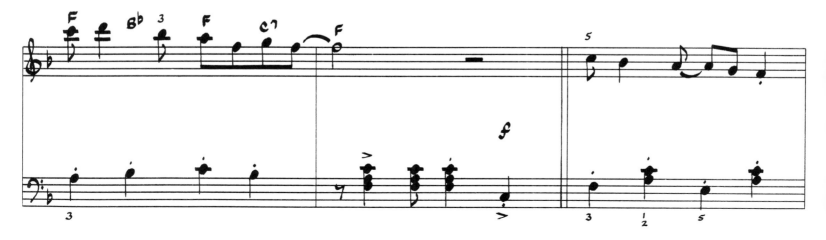

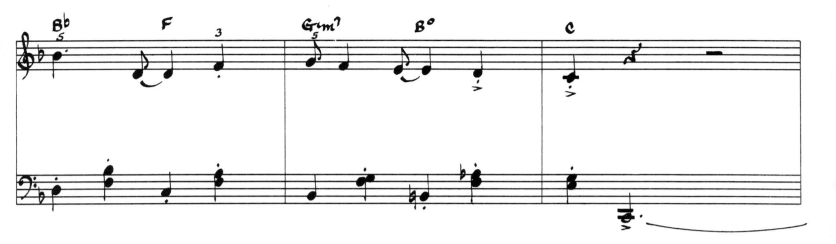

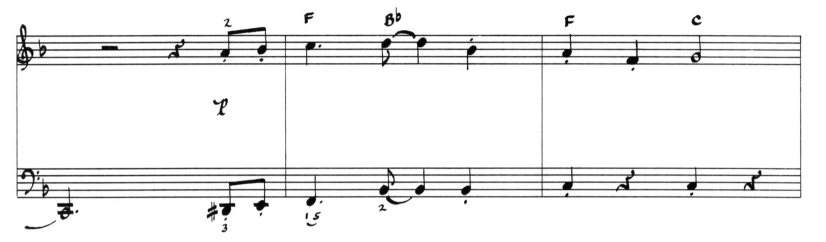

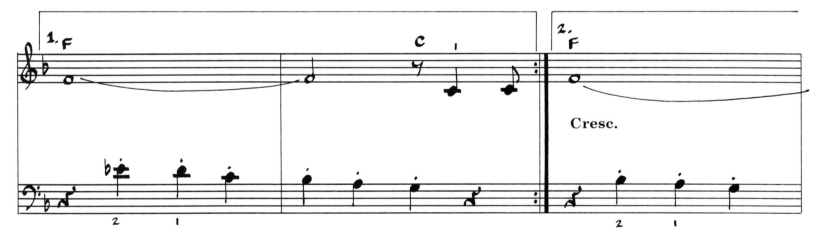

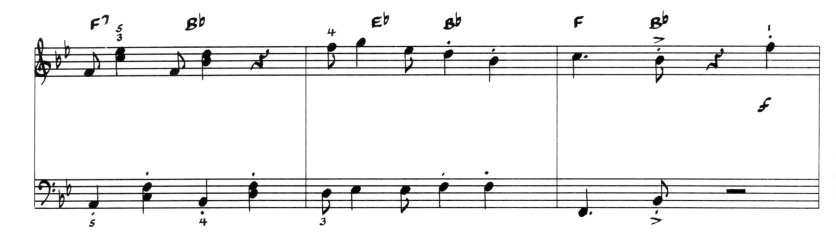

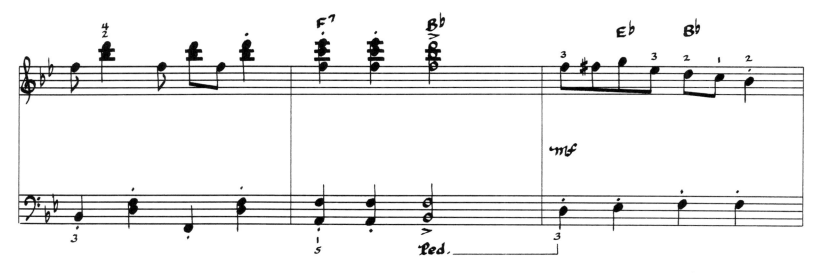

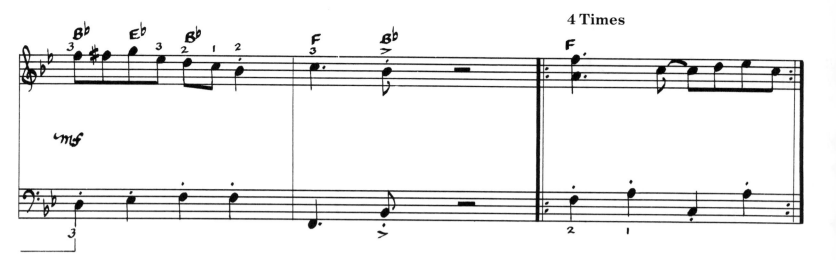

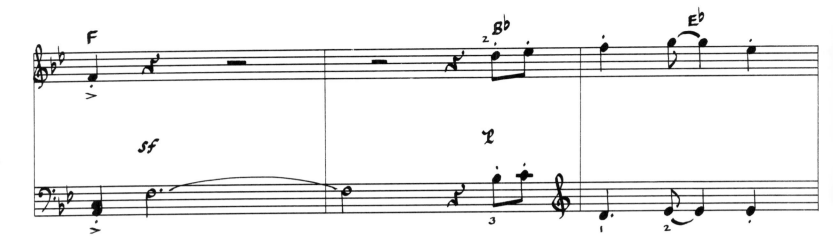

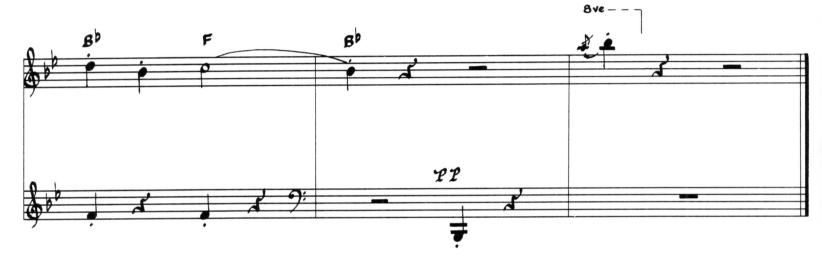

Twelve Days Of Christams

On the first day of Christmas my true love sent to me,
A partridge in a pear tree.
On the second day of Christmas my true love sent to me,
two turlte doves and a partridge in a pear tree.
On the third day of Christmas my true ove sent to me,
Three French hens, Two turtle doves and a partidge in a pear tree.
On the fourth day of Christmas my true love sent to me
Four calling birds, Three French hens, two turtle doves
and a partridge in a pear tree.
On the fifth day of Christmas my true love sent to me,
Five gold rings, Four calling birds, Three French hens
Two turlte doves and a partridge in a pear tree.
On the*

6. Six geese a-laying
7. Seven swans a-swimming
8. Eight maids a-milking
9. Nine ladies dancing
10. Ten lords a-leaping
11. 'Leven pipers piping
12. Twelve drummers drumming

5. Five gold rings
4. Four calling birds
3. Three French hens
2. Two turtle doves, and
   a partridge, etc.

*This section to be played for verses 6 through 12-"On the sixth day",
  "On the seventhe day", etc.

Up On The Housetop

Festively

B. R. Hanby
Arranged by Brian Dykstra

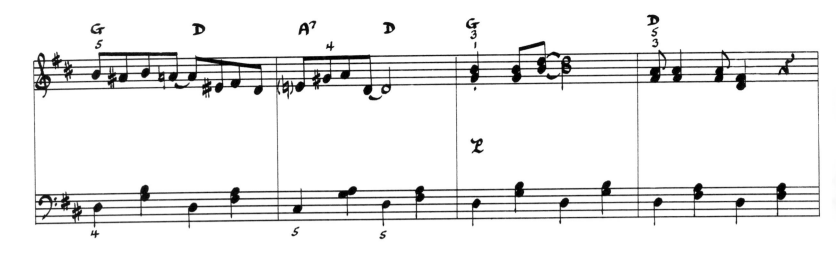

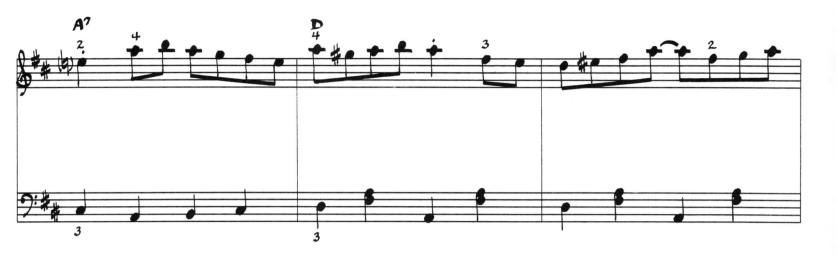

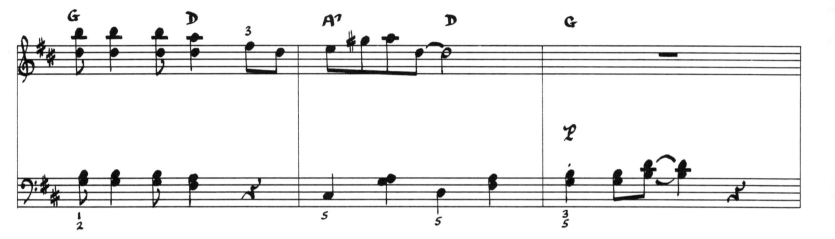

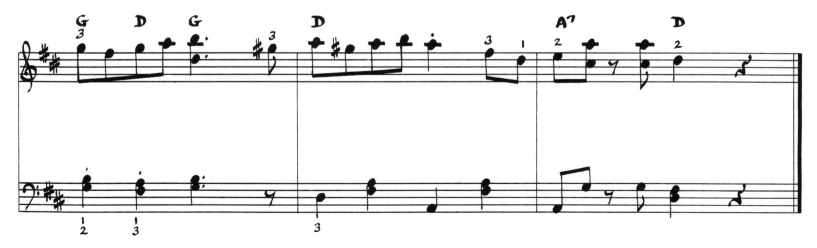

We Wish You A Merry Christmas

Happily

Traditional English Carol
Arranged by Brian Dykstra

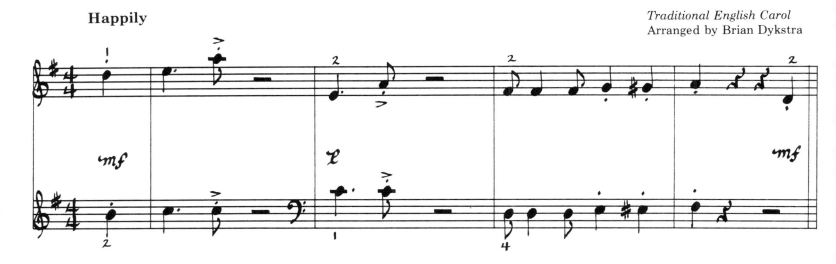

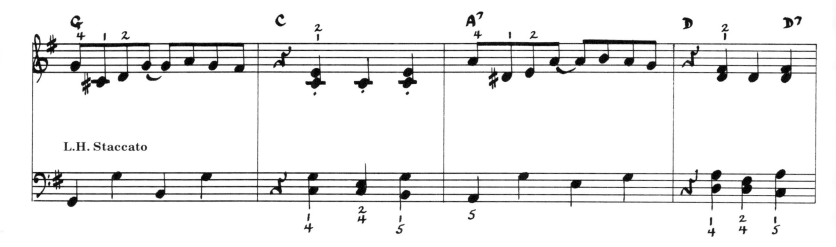

L.H. Staccato

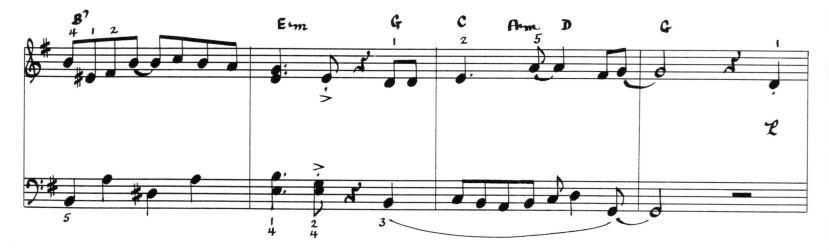

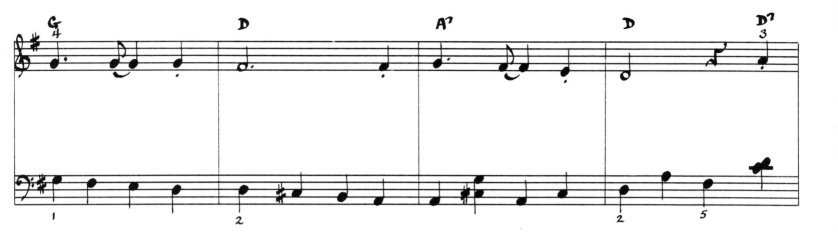

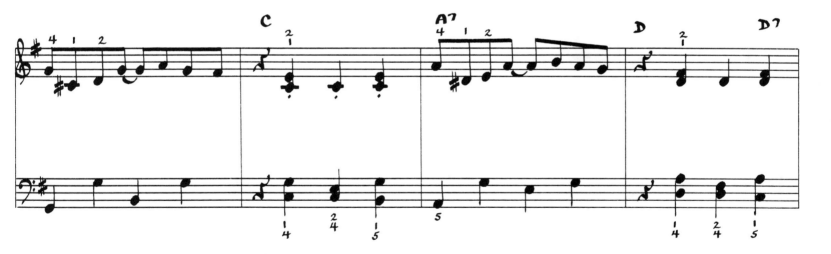

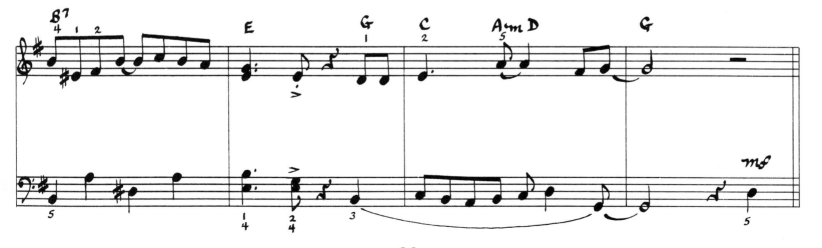

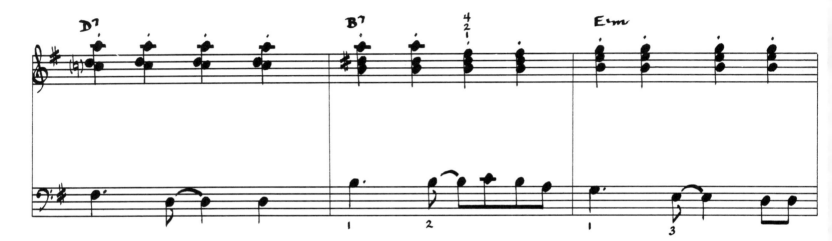

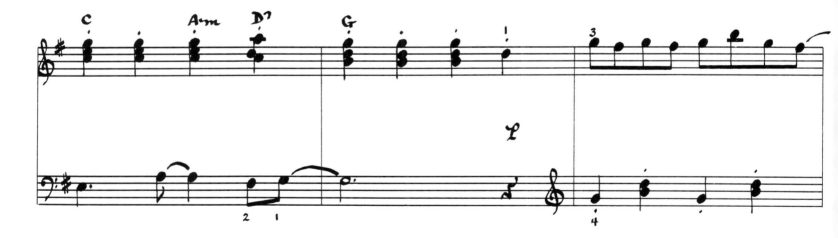

40

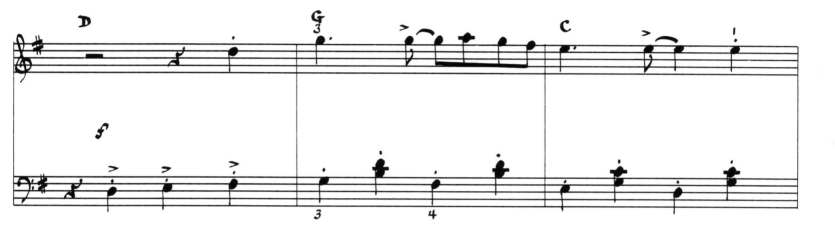

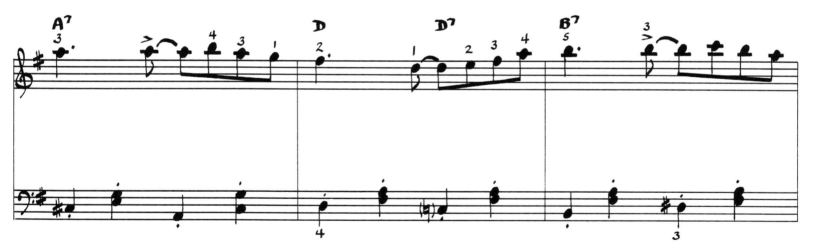

Up on the Housetop

1. Up on the housetop the reindeer pause,
   Out jumps good old Santa Claus;
   Down thro' the chimney with lots of toys,
   All for the little ones' Christmas joys.

   Refrain:
   Ho, ho, ho! Who wouldn't go! Ho, ho, ho! Who wouldn't go!
   Up on the house tip click, click, click,
   Down thro' the chimney with good Saint Nick.

1. First, comes the stocking of little Nell;
   Oh, dear Sants, fill it well;
   Give her a dolly that laughs and cries
   One that will open and shut her eyes.
   Refrain:

3. Next, comes the stocking of little Will;
   Oh, just see what a glorious fill!
   Here is a hammer and lots of tacks,
   Also a ball and whip that cracks.

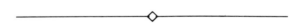

We Wish You A Merry Christmas

1. We wish you a Merry Christmas,
   We wish you a Merry Christmas,
   We wish you a Merry Christams,
   And a Happy New Year!

   Refrain:
   Glad tidings we bring
   To you and your kin;
   Glad tidings for Christmas
   And a Happy New Year!

2. Please bring us some figgy pudding,
   Please bring us some figgy pudding,
   Please bring us some figgy pudding,
   Please bring it right here! Refrain:

3. We wont go until we get some,
   We wont go until we get some,
   We wont go until we get some,
   Please bring it right here!

4. We wish you a Merry Christams,
   We wish you a Merry Christmas,
   We wish you a Merry Christmas,
   And a Happy New Year! Refrain: